Poems From the Crucible

52 For You

By Dean Schoen

Thank you for taking this journey of faith with me

Dean Schoen

© 2010 by Dean Schoen
All right reserved

No part of this book may be reproduced without the written permission of the author.

ISBN: 978-0-578-05392-9

Other book by Dean Schoen:
Study Skills From the Inside

To Contact the Author
DeanSchoen@chartermi.net

Cover design by
Walt Hamilton

What I offer here is a collection of poems, almost all of which were written during my wife's struggle with breast cancer. They begin with our finding a church home and our return to Christ, and then continue throughout the year until Christmas. I intended that they be read one poem per week as devotionals. They speak of our spiritual life as well as our experience within our church family. My prayer is that they may be a blessing to you.

This poem celebrates what came to be our familiar drive to church, and our welcome into our new church family.

Warmups

The week is punctuated by
That turn at the gas station,
Then down the street into
The parking lot, already
Looking for that first wave or
Smile.
Greeted at the door,
Reeled into the building by handshake,
Searching for little connections:
Babies packaged in love and
Bundled in the nursery, adult
Handshakes firm and sure, children
Connected everywhere to a second
Family as loving as their own,
Minister greeting and skating
On to another task, rogue notes
Dropped from the music special to
Come, one moment when someone
Stops to mend a hurt, and keep the
Bond tight, and on down the hall, open
To God's game plan
For surprise blessings.

So now you are a Christian, or you have rededicated your life to Christ. How will this change your life?

And Now the Walk

Up from your knees
After accepting Christ,
Enter into a new atmosphere
Of deep breath tied to roots
That both ground and reach
Upward. Will Christ now
Walk with you through times
Of sick children, of possessions
Broken, of food dropped on the floor,
Of losing your job, and through times
Of pride, lust and the chance to
Witness? The answer is yes, and
Yes again, but the needed question is
"Will your grip of His hand
Remain as firm?"

We begin to explore what this new relationship with Christ during troubling times means for us.

Abiding in Him

Abiding in Him
Is to rest, stopping
In gratitude to place
Your burden with Him,
To remain without
Rushing away,
By standing clean in
The center of His love,
And following His shadow
Into sweet stillness.

Abiding in Him is to
Stand firm as a reed in
A storm, connected fast
To the cross, to submit by
Melting from alternatives
Into His path.

Abiding in Him is to
Go on setting your course
By the drawing of His love,
To reside, to set your table
And to find your sanctuary
In His love.

It was not long before our comfort was habitual through worship and being part of a church family.

Here in His Presence

Here is the moment
God has given you.
Take this moment and
Celebrate all its possibilities,
Not drifting into a future
That might not be, that chases
The present and makes it
Disappear. Stay here to find
What He has for you,
What there is to be learned,
To measure your growth.
Stay here with Him now,
See all that He has for you.
It is not in the past where
Lessons were learned and
Celebrations were won,
But here in His presence
Where He can grab hold
Of you and never let go.

We followed the command to profess our faith through water baptism.

Renewed in Water

Will you take this
Test of flattened hair,
Clothes molded to your
Body, showing the
Congregation the meaning
Of obedience by following
The Lord into water,
Eased backwards into
The softness of our Father
And the sweet Comforter, and
Bursting through old dominions
Up, out of the water into the
Arms of Jesus.

Our appreciation of every day of every season grew as well as our love for one another.

Seasonal Voice

Stopping to turn,
I say, "It's as though
I've never seen it before,
This dross of leaves falling
From God's palette
To surround me."

How can I not believe in
Him when He calls me to
Witness this, to know I
Must find Him in moments
Like this or miss the seasonal
Splendor of His voice again
Whispering in my ear.

She may even wave at the window
While I am quiet within the
Swirling leaves. Stalled in this
Requiem for seasonal change,
Bursting on the empty fullness
Of fall, desperate for this certain
Moment of your wife's love,
Knowing she waits just beyond
The walls. For this moment you
Can be complete in God's loving
Reminder of life's brevity,
And in knowing He has provided
Sanctuary just beyond the door.

We took delight in watching the children grow into their faith.

Seeds

Legs sticking straight
Out from the pews,
The little ones squirm
And fidget. From side
To side the marble rolls
Within them. The boys,
Hands stuffed in pockets,
White shirts hanging out
Of their pants, girls making
Long eye contact, seeing
What adults don't. But one
Focused idea from God's
Word makes its way through
Their dispersed senses,
Slipping through the almost
Stillness, finding a place to
Rest, and it blooms in the
Cement of adult life.

A devotional life throughout the week allows God to be a presence in our lives.

Directing Your Steps

Spend time in prayer
And God will plan your day.
He will make connections
Not seen, arrange steps
You cannot plan, refresh
In ways you do not know.
Set your compass toward Him,
And pull Him toward you
Through your prayer.
Pathways may seem unclear,
But His blood can trace
The route to your heart.
During the silence between
Your words in prayer,
His plan is already at work,
And you may call upon Him
When you are lost.

To find our pastor to be a man of God and to find his door and heart open to us during my wife's terminal illness gave us comfort and support.

A Pastor's Heart

A pastor's heart moves
Like a conductor's wand
To the winds of change
Within his church, his
Attention fixed on Jesus
With loving diversions to
Those in need. He must
Linger with them in
Loneliness, and stand firm
With them in their fears.
He casts the message of
God's word to plant and
Renew as the reach of
His heart sweeps over
All the generation's ever
Shifting needs, his heart
A plumb line to the emotions
Of his people in joy, in
Sorrow, and in need.

Our church is small enough to allow us to see the source of pastor's heart was a continual and earnest prayer life.

A Pastor's Time Alone

A pastor's time alone
Folds back over his
Needs to husk down
To what is firm and true
For him and for others.
He locates Jesus for himself,
And then directs others
To the correct path, to search
God's word for a trail that
Leads to a banquet.

While on his knees, he
Must pray to help others
Sift through the confusion
To clarity. He will leave his
Knees as he ends his search
For the lightning of the Word,
And for the place where people
Can rest beyond the compassion
Of a pastor's love into the truth
Of God's love.

As a cancer patient, life awaits the next cat-scan, and the need to trust God's hand as one waits for the results.

Reclaiming Your Joy

Can you find
Joy again on the
Path you now walk?
Do you know God's
Hand is sure as ever,
His grip not loosened
As you regain your balance.

As you go down this path,
Not able to see around
The next corner, He will
Nudge you forward,
To find joy waiting for
You, more wonderful
Because you thought it gone.

Amid all the alternatives and plans during the illness, which cause exhaustion of reason, the Holy Spirit was our resting place.

The Holy Spirit

The Holy Spirit
Guides faith on its
Path to the heart,
And offers sanctuary
To an exhausted reason
That adds why to
Every question and
Hesitates in defiance
Of a truce, while faith
Stands and offers its peace.

At times I would think back to the day when we found out the cancer was back, and what that was like before coming back to Christ.

Blindsided

Striding through life
And without warning,
You smack your head
On a disease like an
Unseen rafter. Spiraling
Down that question mark,
There is only uncertainty in
Looking for answers, no
Pathway, no real experience
Until you fall back within
Yourself, until you find
Jesus near your heart,
To be asked in, and end
Your search for answers
From the inside.

I wrote this poem after my wife received chemo in the same room with a young mother with terminal cancer, who was also receiving chemo, and who talked of her young daughter's questions about God.

Who is There?

A child says to her mother,
" I don't think God is
Listening to our prayers."
From a child's eyes
A mother's sickness may
Seem too big for God's
Arms to surround. Now
Is when God reaches out
And embraces you even
More closely with His
Love and His love shared
Through others. Now when
You most need it, look
Into your mother's eyes,
And you will find no
Blame or hatred passed
On to you. She would
Only say her dreams have
Already been met because
You are her child.

Easter morning was fresher and newer than it had ever been as we had renewed hope in our savior.

Easter Morning

On that morning
Mary peered into
The tomb, finding
The surprise and joy
Of the emptiness
That sealed our salvation.
The emptiness of the tomb
Filled her heart with the
Certainty of a redeemer.
Her shout of empty
Echoes down through
The time when each man's
Heart must find its foundation.
Now blinded by His absence,
But not yet seeing that from
This time forward, we will
Never be alone.

We got the answer to the question of how married life could be different when in a relationship with Christ.

Couples in Christ

He is both with you
And beyond both of
You, your source above
The tension and the
Clarifier of communication
That draws the beauty
Of two joined voices up
To Him, offering the comfort
Of His spiritual harness, drawing
By His grace both of you
In the same direction as
You walk in and out of church,
Pray over your meals, and
Pursue your separate ministries,
Joined in Christ, and working
Toward the same glory of Him.

The contrast is easy to see in a married life without Christ.

Couples Without Christ

And you thought
It would be so easy
When you could do
Nothing but delight
One another, now even
The amount of sugar
You spoon must be
Defended as you play
Bumper cars throughout
Your married life and
Race on to your next
Collision. This ride can
End abruptly these days
With two people surrendering
Their bond. Frayed and bruised,
You forgot Jesus can stop
The compass from spinning
And assure you through
Cracks and faults into the
Comfort of His guidance,
The gravity within your
Bond that keeps it true.

Sitting in Sunday school, someone pretended to complain about his life, and he began to instruct the Lord about his troubles, and those comments fell into place as a poem.

If You Knew, Oh Lord

If You knew, oh Lord, how hard it is
For me to live for You, You would
Understand my failure.

If You knew, Lord, how success eludes
Me, You would ease my frustration.

If You knew, oh Lord, other's expectations
You would not hold me to Yours.

If You knew, Lord, my responsibility,
You would not add Yours.

If You knew, oh Lord, the abuse I have
Suffered, You would bless me.

But, of course, You know, and You wait
For my response.

In attending the church, it did not take long to appreciate the vital role women play in the church body.

Women's Ministries

Because their feelings go
Deeper in not forgetting
What men may forget,
Women's hearts reach out
To the congregation's needs.
They fill the sanctuary with
Voices that harmonize
With the angels in song
And in solo, and then teach
The children on laps of love
About their Redeemer.
They answer the call for
Meals when people most
Need uplifting grace.
First at the altar, giving
In feminine touch and prayer
The comfort needed, and
At service end, they weave
A pattern of love up the
Aisle from side to side
Through the congregation,
Stopping to minister to
One more need before leaving.

This poem celebrates the return to Christ after temporarily wandering off course.

So Right

Slipping far enough
From Christ to find
Our minds wandering
Into strange harbors
Outside the circle of His
Grace, left to navigate
From our own maps, and
Then, suddenly,
We connect to God's
Grace, as it gathers us
Into His presence, placing
Us where everything is so
Right, so sweetly aligned
To His favor that nothing,
Nothing is out of place,
Where our hearts secure
The memory of closeness
That will last through our lives.

At no time is pride ever completely defeated in the church or anywhere else.

Pride

And there it is again,
That pride, putting self
First, lurking behind
Humility, taking satisfaction
Where it does no good. When
We connect with others and
Are threatened, must we lose
Life if not in victory?
Such a familiar journey, why
Cannot pride be shown its
Proper seat? We travel
Through life with pride
Following us as a tail
Stepped on by the world.
Pride marks us and assures us,
And we protect it as a tail curled
Around us, but can we see when
The soft curl becomes hard?

And then there are those times when one is absolutely lost in the glory of the Holy Spirit.

Soaring in the Spirit

The Holy Spirit is God's hand
Reaching down to pull us up
As we reach up to pull Him
Close, and somewhere in the middle
We stand soaring in the Spirit.
We embrace the flood of His grace
That, were it not measured, would
Stun us by His glory.

Into His glory, we shed everything
Except our senses, each picking
Its own route into His Holy Spirit.
Into the eye of His Spirit, we may
See as a jewel in a sunbeam,
Into the sound of His Spirit, we
May whisper into the ear of God,
And as the Holy Spirit saturates, we
Feel the reason for our existence.

It as a great blessing for my wife to find people praying for healing at times and under circumstances that were not always convenient.

Intercession

On your knees alone at work among
The packages in the storeroom,
Forced there by your connection
To someone in need of your prayers.
It is not pity, this urge to carry
Their need to the mercy seat,
To drop out of your bed at three a.m.,
More awake than you have every been,
To reach out and up to be that person's
Advocate, on your knees,
And on your face.

In church, so burdened you must go
To the person, knowing by the Spirit's
Leading that you can't live if you don't
Help that person carry the load for a day,
Or forever, and the rest comes only
After the struggle is joined.

God's call within the body of believers remains a challenge in moving forward spiritually, especially when cancer is part of one's life.

God's Call

God's call comes for me,
And how does it come for you?
Is it inside you like the quiet
Summer afternoon before the first
Drops of rain are felt
On your upturned face?

Or is it the singe of Jesus' blood
That burns through your temples,
Or is it the wind of the Holy Spirit
Twisting inside you?

Because we hesitate, someone else
May answer, and we are left wondering
If He will ever call again.

God's spirit pushes at our boundaries,
Splashing at the tops of our resistance,
Resistance holding us back as the pebble
Beneath the wheel of the stalled car that
Won't be moved and can't be started.

The chance passes from the Holy Spirit's
Burrowing within us
In search of permission,
Withdrawing only a short distance
And waiting.

I attended, upon my wife's encouragement, a men's advance, and was moved by the passion of the men in prayer for one another.

Men Gathering in Christ

Funneled into one place,
250 men gathered in doubles,
And triples, forehead to forehead,
Mining the Holy Spirit, crying
And shaking, holding up one
Another's hands, surrounding
The exposed hearts, sore from
Abuse and neglect, bracing them
With joy of the Holy Spirit.

The man behind me shouts
" Come on" to the minister
He wants to go all the way
In worship to explore new gifts
And old ashes and to encourage
Freedom to worship God in a roar
That is a balm leading back through
All the hallways of pain and disappointment
That led to this place.

Doubt, like pride, will always be there, but it can lead to a deeper faith, ever with a bad Cat-scan report

Doubt

Doubt can strangle
Our purchase of grace,
Blighting our comfort
And trust, but if we know
It as a tool to prune and
Cultivate a deeper faith,
It need not destroy our
Harvest. It can deepen
Our roots and multiply
Our yield.

The question of revival is always present, and what does it take for that to happen? We watched as that question was continually raised.

Fit and Responsible

There is faith that leads
And faith that leads higher,
And we hope to be judged
Fit and responsible for His
Promised outpouring; rubbed
By the hours of feeling the carpet
Against our knees and faces,
Ransacking our lives for fault
And repentance, begging for
The shower to be poured out
As it flows from our salvation
Through Jesus; to reach out and
Up, Grasping with both hands,
And when our hands come down, still
Be in touch with the sweep of the
Holy Spirit that rallies our souls
In the hungry pursuit of God's blessings.

What a struggle it is for us sometimes to concentrate in our pursuit of Christ, although cancer has the ability to focus our attention.

Distractions

We are a fan of distractions,
One thought rippling into another,
Spread wide to pull and
Stretch us away from Jesus,
But as we fold the fan back
And hold it by the base,
We are at our source, Jesus,
Who provides all our life.
And then we may choose to spread
The fan in gratitude. For distractions
Can be opportunities binding us
To Jesus when we raise our arm
To fan the winds of the Holy Spirit
Within us.

Missionaries would often visit the church, whether getting ready to go into the field or coming back, and their dedication deeply moved us.

The Missionary

There is no strength
To carry the world's needs
In your heart without God's
Calling. Planted in their soil,
You present Christ's love
As it sifts through the barrier
Of words into their hearts.
How far inside do you go
In facing the landscape of
Frustration you will find?

Those you will find will
Look far inside you to see
If there is enough for them
To change a thousand years
Of belief. How much joy
Can be contained when they
Come to Christ so deeply
And without doubt that healing
Can be instant and complete?

So if you have heard God's call, how will you pursue it?

Obedience

When God's grace settles
Deeply within, your faith
Can move forward to meet
His expectations, now finding
Your stroke after first drifting
Into His deep waters.

You read of the Israelite's
Lack of obedience and wonder
How could they disobey
With God there with them?
You know that God is here
Even as your back stiffens
During His request, but doubt
Lessens in each step of faith,
And as you stand in solitude
With God, you know His will
Can be done in you.

This poem addresses those places we still hold on to; strongholds that even salvation is not permitted to change.

Deep Harbors

There are places
So deeply hid, you
Would be surprised
To find them if you
Searched, places you
Didn't give to Jesus
Because they are the
Mystery of who you
Are, harbors closed
Even to the balm of
Salvation. These are
The regions where
God's grace must work
The hardest to change
Mistrust to love,
Ridicule to nurture,
And anger to joy.
God's grace must
Peel through these
Layers to open a new
View to clouded eyes.

Oh, those hurt feelings that cause people to withdraw and even leave the body of believers.

Sensitivity

The spin of my world
Can be tilted by a careless
Word when the equation
Of the two of us leaves
The depth of my ruins
Unknown amid the
Stickiest of words
That do not easily
Fall away.

In talk my beliefs
Bubble up like
An artesian well
That is my life.
Can I find that person
Who is the flint to my
Stone, burning with
The same air of concern
In a single light of appreciation,
Or in talk that turns to lead,
Can I preserve my weakness
With a gentle callous that
Filters through to love?

How does one deal with the issue of healing when there has been prayer and healing does not happen?

Whose Way

Yes, you want to be
Healed instantly
With all the flesh
Renewed so quickly
That news is carried from
Lip to lip. You know God
Is listening, and He may
Yet heal your way, but
You want an answer,
And to provide the
Instructions to riddles
Only God understands.
The growth and learning
During this would not
Be because you already
Have all the answers
To God's mysteries.

Here is this Biblical commandment to pray for one another in this way.

Laying on of Hands

Lighten your soul
And present yourself
To another for prayer,
By entering a womb of
Closeness as another
Reaches out to touch you
And call upon Jesus' name.
With the oil of prayer and
The sweet Comforter, your
Burdens slake off as that
Friend takes your name
To Jesus, leading to the
Mercy Seat, and the touch
Continues until your quaking
Turns into firmer ground.

To never lose that connection to pray for others is part of a Christian's life.

Connected

May there be a core
Of concern continuing
To pass through me
So that the burdens
Of others stir me to action
In prayer to ease their
Feeling of loneliness from
Carrying something heavy
For too long. Let the line
That connects us grow light
And vibrate with those needs
So my prayer feeds back to
Them about another reaching
Out on their behalf to Jesus
Not once, but as steadily
As that line is secure.

So many times, as the Holy Spirit moved throughout the service, new levels of intimacy attained would carry us through another week.

Explore

Fall back into the
Surrounding presence
Of God, be carried by
His grace, be lifted by the
Holy Spirit, suspending
You and moving you toward
The goal already reached,
Of your praise flowing
Into His love.

When we would hear of miraculous healing, often in primitive cultures, we would wonder what is happening there that makes it possible.

Questions

What number of days,
Still and quiet in God's
Presence, would dissolve
The veneer of life holding
Us back from the miracles
Of healing? Could we ever fear
Less the mystery of multiplying cells?

Could we stand as naked in innocence
As the native in Africa listening
To the gospel? Are the natives'
Miracles a gift that deepens
Their faith, or is their faith deeper
Than ours? Do they know gratitude
Where we find only spectacle?
Just a fly in Pascal's room disrupted
His prayer, but we carry more
Distractions in thick bundles that
Keep us from standing naked as
That native without a Bible
Who finds God's miracles.

Unlocking the treasures of the Bible in daily devotions became a part of our life.

Conduit

Nosing around in
The Bible, looking
For the passage that
Creates a circuit that
Connects in all directions
To God's purpose, hoping
It is understood as it was
Meant to be, a holy web
Walked through that sticks
Through a lifetime.

Perhaps that question of why healing does not take place gets some answers in this poem.

The Other Miracle

What is the miracle
Before healing, if not
To appear before God
With the faith of a child,
Stripped bare of bank accounts,
Stock reports, credit cards
Intellectual doubts,
Denominational differences,
Or fear of another's opinions,
But to present one's
Self with culture cast aside,
Shucked and stripped to a
Complete faith so that grace
Meets only your need, not
Your defenses?

In the struggle with cancer, one does not want the connection to Christ to grow weak.

Disconnect

When the world has
Released your hand,
And your reach seems
Not long enough to
Reconnect, and if you
Were able to touch,
It may not touch back.
You may want to fold
Within yourself and
Hope to change into
Something better. If
There is not enough life
In you to push back
To the life that is, you
May open yourself to Christ
Who will touch you and
Reconnect you in ways
You did not think possible.

This poem tells of how my wife dealt with breast cancer and the effect it had on others, including those who were observers and those who shared the experience of cancer.

God's Grace in Laura

In a room filled
With faces without the
Color of life, you do not
Search deeply to find
God's grace living in Laura's
Smile as she goes into the
Room for another treatment.
Could you mirror Laura's love
If you go through the doubt of
Disease that could cause
You to walk away from
God's face. The people in
Her church fast and pray,
Making their quilt of faith
And love because they see
Her faith and love in God.
Can you believe it possible
To fall even deeper in love
With Jesus if he says to you,
"I can not stop what is happening
To you, but I will make it as easy
For you as I can?"

The closer you are to Christ, the clearer his directions will be.

Directions

Someone said if
You spend enough
Time in prayer,
God will plan your day.

He will make connections
You don't see, arrange stops
You cannot plan, refresh you
In ways you do not know.

He will set your compass
Toward Him, and pull you
Toward His path

In the silence between
Your words, He traces the
Prayer that leads to your heart,
And when His blood renews
Your heart, your answer will be
To leave your past and follow Him.

God can provide answers if we are available.

Solutions

The solutions flutter in
Front of you like ribbons
In the wind, and you look
For God's strong signal among
The flashing lights of indecision.
You think the solution is yours,
But do not want the debt or error.
In the struggle to quiet confusion,
You want God to jolt you into clarity,
To roar "Do this!" But as you listen,
His answer may come in folds within
The laundry basket, or a turn completed
On the highway home, where Jesus can
Swell your heart to certainty with the
Comfort of His calling.

The miracle of salvation occurs again an(
as new believers become part of a congre

Breaking Down

The salvation message comes
And pieces begin to fall as
We thrash about to rebuild
And to keep Jesus out.
Once He is inside
Our fortress, we must release
Control, and be rebuilt
Not by our hands, but His.
When we can't replace the
Barricades as fast as the
Droplets of His grace
Shower us, we accept the
Flood of His new design,
Now on higher ground.
Never has it been so good
To lose this battle
To a stronger love.

This poem was written earlier as a tribute to my grandfather, a retired minister.

Bonded

During the stillness in time
When a change in weather is
Sensed, an old man seated on
A bus is connected to the
World by his wife, a knot to
Keep him from falling away.

Before grandfather got old,
He smelled of cologne and
Wool, carpet thick in his
Overcoat; he wore a bowler
Hat when gathering our
Family with arms veined
And too muscular for a
Preacher. He taught me
How to eat banana splits
Faster than anyone as we
Spooned chocolate puddles
Past strawberries, leaving
The bananas for last. Grand-
Father ransacked us with
Tenderness, the pricklings
Of his mustache a memory
When rubbing my beard.

(Continued...)

When grandfather got old,
He would journey through
Years, leaving thick despair
Behind. His eyes
Opened from a place where
Nothing changed, his voice
A metronome that paced our
Wanderings through his youth.

How do we decide in light of God's leading our lives, and when do we find certainty?

Signs

We want directions
Out of the darkness.
We pray to the Lord
For those ribbons in
The wind, lining up
Day after day, pointing
In the same direction.
But where is the assurance
When they go in opposite
Directions?

Can you recall the last time
You felt certain? Did it blossom
Slowly, nourished by
Droplets until you felt the
Shower all over you,
And did it not matter
That you were in the middle
Of a storm? Can we be alert
To know the Lord's prompting,
To see his signs as we go,
And not to see them for
The first time when the
Journey is over.

A member of the congregation asked me if I was mad at God because of the cancer, and I answered in this poem.

Thank You for This Good Day

> The blur of life
> Sometimes halts
> To a single frame,
> And that moment
> Settles upon you,
> Pulling you deeply
> Into it, to be fully
> Awake to the stream
> Of blessings that pass
> Through us, to stand in
> Front of a mirror of
> Appreciation, feeling
> All the parts within
> You that are good,
> For all God has done
> For you in this day
> And days passed.
> God stops you to say
> This moment will never
> Exist again, to be appreciated
> Now, soon then only as a
> Memory. Expand yourself
> And express your thanks
> Back to Him.

To watch the eldest members of the congregation, who had served Christ the longest, was a great blessing.

Old Saint

An old saint moves
Down the aisle as the
Spiritual glue of the
Church, his eyes sparkling
Beneath the gray hair,
He carries this church
Forward through humility,
As he journeys through the
Years with Jesus. His respect
Shows in his brushed hair
And pressed suit, only the
Best for Jesus. There is no
Moodiness, his ministry is
His smile, and his years of
Prayer, gathered as a monument
To what a spiritual life can be.

It is always a challenge to allow bitterness over life's problems to hinder one's spiritual life.

Expectations

And did you expect
The road after your
Salvation to provide
A bridge over every stream,
And pavement instead
Of gravel?

Was your expectation keeping
You in prayer, and in the Word,
Or did your relationship with Jesus
Become a quiz show with you
Clapping your hands,
Asking for more?

How did you come to expect
So many benefits from giving
So little of yourself? If bitterness
Is the result, you have only
To reach up and find Jesus hand
Reaching down from the Cross
To pull you safely forward.

We came to our church when there was a national revival going on, and there was a desire to have the same experience locally.

Reaching for Revival

Standing there, hands
Outstretched, asking for
The Holy Spirit to be God's
Flint in striking a fire
That lasts over time. You
Want to stand with cupped
Hands, accepting the overflow
Of God's grace, but have you
Prayed your passage to fitness
Through years of cleansing
Repentance?

What is your service to Him?
Are you examined and ready?
Can you run the long race?
Can you prepare the table
For those coming to be fed?
God does not want an
Embarrassed people with
No vessels to receive His grace.

How beautiful is the Christmas season when Christ is helping us through the struggle with cancer.

The Birth of Jesus

You will not find Him
Among the wispy ribbons,
Among the aisles packed
With shoppers, or among
The light, lacy lines pulled
From your roof.

Did you, as a child, find
Him when you first saw
A manger and felt His
Birth for the world, a
Compass from despair to
Hope? Did you see the child,
Like you, helpless in a world,
But with the power to redeem
All mankind?

Do you carry Him within
Your heart on Christmas Eve
As you travel from the church
To the heart of your family?
And as you sing " Holy Night,"
Do you find His presence pouring
Into the mold inside your heart?

It is all about Him.

Beholding the Christ as a Child

In the manger lies the fragile
Figurine of Jesus, and as a child,
I am drawn to Him, and I join
Those who look with curiosity
And wonder, recognizing that
It is all about Him, and He may
Become the focus of my life,
The beginning of a promise
That will not break as this figurine
Could, that will provide an eternal
Comfort for those who come
To know Him as I found Him.